ROUNDS WITH
A COUNTRY VET

ROUNDS WITH
A COUNTRY VET

TEXT AND PHOTOGRAPHS BY

Richard B. McPhee

Dodd, Mead & Company *New York*

1 2 3 4 5 6 7 8 9 10

Library of Congress Cataloging in Publication Data
McPhee, Richard B
   Rounds with a country vet.

   SUMMARY: Text and photos follow a country veterinarian
as he cares for the animals of his rural area. Describes
various animal diseases and their treatment.
   1. Veterinary medicine—Pictorial works—Juvenile
literature. 2. Beneke, George J. 3. Veterinarians—
New York (State)—Biography—Juvenile literature.
[1. Veterinary medicine. 2. Beneke, George J.
3. Veterinarians] I. Title.
SF756.M3   636.089   77-6496
ISBN 0-396-07482-0

For Charlotte,
who always leads the way

ROUNDS WITH
A COUNTRY VET

Introduction

If you have ever had the experience of meeting someone and knowing right off—without quite knowing why—that he or she is your friend, then you'll know exactly how I felt the day that I first met George Beneke, DVM. Doctor of Veterinary Medicine.

It was a cold, snowy Sunday morning in early February, almost three years ago now. I was going through a period of great uncertainty in my life. I had no clear sense of purpose. One day two friends of mine invited me to spend some time with them at their cabin in the woods. "A cabin in the woods . . . " What a magical phrase! I felt that in such an isolated and natural setting, free from the stresses of city life, I might find it easier to get back in touch with myself. If I could find myself, then perhaps I could find a purpose for my life. By going back to nature, a more natural order of things, perhaps I might more clearly begin to see how I belonged. I accepted my friends' generous offer.

On that particular Sunday in February, we had gotten up early, with the first light and our animals, to take a walk in the falling snow. We cut across the mountain that rose behind the cabin and stopped to visit Otto, a neighbor, a couple of miles away. Two of Otto's dogs

9

were sick. He was waiting for the vet, cussing the cold—and just about everything else. I think it was Otto's way of keeping warm.

As we stood and talked, a truck slowly made its way toward us through the heavily falling snow. As it came closer, Otto recognized it as the Mobile Veterinary Clinic for which he had been waiting. Out jumped George Beneke. He seemed enormous to me at that moment, partly because I was feeling pretty small and partly because George *is* well over six feet and well over two hundred pounds. He was full of good spirits and didn't seem to mind at all that it was 8:30 on Sunday morning.

For the next few minutes I was totally fascinated as I watched George carefully examine and treat Otto's pups. After giving shots and prescribing precise future care, he closed his case and reached into the cab of the mobile clinic, lifting his young son Chris into his arms—by way of a proud introduction. At two and a half, Chris already liked to ride along with his daddy just as much as his daddy clearly liked to have him along. The two-way radio in the cab of the mobile beeped. Another emergency call. George and Chris were off, disappearing as they had come, into the still falling snow.

I sensed immediately that something very special had just happened to me. Instinctively I felt that it might be part of the discovery that I had come to the country to make. All that day my mind kept returning to the scene . . . the snow, the mobile clinic, and George Beneke, DVM.

I wasn't working at the time. That was one of the many uncertainties in my life. So a few days later I contacted George at the Copake Veterinary Hospital and asked, feeling somewhat foolish, if I could follow him around, ride along with him on his rounds for a month or so. I told him I was willing to work, to help or assist him in any way

10

that I could. I asked only that I might bring my camera along. George agreed; I think he sensed it was something I needed to do.

I went back to New York City to get a few things together and make preparations for a month in the country. The city brought back a lot of self-doubts and I almost abandoned the project. But I kept remembering the power and excitement that I had felt that Sunday morning. So on April 11, I loaded the VW with camera, typewriter, assorted supplies and animals (my great dane, Charlotte, and cat, "Chick"), and headed back to the cabin in the woods. It was late evening as I approached Hillsdale, the little town nearest the cabin, and it was snowing. The snow seemed like an omen, reminding me of the moment when I had first met George.

It was nearly midnight and the long, winding hill to the cabin proved icy and treacherous. I was ready to panic. It was storming, so dark I couldn't see five feet in front of me—and I still had two miles to go. Charlotte bounded from the stranded car, delighted with the snow, and headed in the direction of the cabin. She knew the way, as she always does. I tucked Chick inside my coat and set off after Charlotte. With every step I wondered what I had gotten myself into this time. It took us all a good hour in front of a blazing fire to thaw out.

The following day dawned sunny and much warmer. By noon the road to the cabin had been plowed and I began to feel better. I spent the rest of the day settling in at the cabin and preparing to meet George at the veterinary hospital in nearby Copake Falls at 8:00 the next morning.

I arrived at the hospital about 7:30. I guess I wanted to prove to George that a city boy could get up early and be on time. I was full of emotion, excited by the adventure that was about to begin. I was also apprehensive about my ability to measure up to it. It was colder again, so I got out of the VW and sat on the rail fence in the sun to wait.

Minutes later a station wagon drove up to the parking area with a calf stretched out in the back. There was a terrible stillness about the calf, and I knew that it was dead. That was not the way I wanted this day to begin. It was almost 8:00 now. The hospital phone began to ring in the distance. And then George arrived in the mobile clinic. Almost immediately he began to examine the dead calf. According to the young farmer it had been born alive and apparently healthy just hours before. It had taken a sudden turn and the farmer had rushed for the hospital. It died on the way. He wanted to know why, as we always want to know why—not that it ever changes anything.

As George turned to the clinic to get an autopsy knife, he spoke to me for the first time. He told me not to be embarrassed if I didn't feel like watching. All my fears and doubts were right there in my mouth at that moment, ready to spill out on the ground. But I had come to see and to learn, and this was the beginning that was presented to me.

George returned his concentration to the calf. He carefully slit it open from throat to stomach. I remember being surprised that there was so little blood; I had expected it to come gushing out from everywhere. Methodically, George located and examined the vital organs, one by one. I watched, unable to move or turn away. I even recognized a few of them—the heart, the liver, the kidneys. I followed George's enormous hands until eventually he found the cause, a ruptured bladder and vessels, probably the result of the mother's unusually severe labor contractions. It was a sad moment. When there was nothing more to say, George turned and headed for the hospital and the persistently ringing phone.

12

George works in partnership with two other veterinarians, Drs. Murray Jenkins and Paul Layer. As a team, they operate the Veterinary Hospital in Copake Falls, New York. They are essentially a large animal practice and serve the surrounding farms and communities within a twenty-five to thirty-five mile radius, the rural dairy and beef farms and horse stables of New York, Massachusetts, and Connecticut.

In the morning the doctors gather at the hospital at 8:00 A.M. with their mobile clinics, to take morning calls and set up the day's rounds. Eighty percent of their time is spent in the field and on the road. Office hours at the hospital for pets and small animals that can be brought in are between 1:00 and 2:00 P.M. Emergencies are handled by two-way radio contact between the hospital and the mobiles . . . "Mobile Two to K Double E, 514—Over," and at least one doctor is always on duty, twenty-four hours a day, seven days a week.

Everything was new to me. I was born and raised in the city. I had taken a few nature walks as a kid and spent a few weekends in the country. My father, like many city fathers, always dreamed of having a little farm in the country one day. But we didn't get much closer than the dreams. Now I was beginning to experience life and work in the country as it really is. There was so much for me to absorb, and in the first days I remember being overwhelmingly impressed with the strenuous physical demands of George's life and work.

Although I have ridden with George on many occasions in the past three years, I have never forgotten the wonders of that first day. It was an astonishing sight to watch George stick a sleeved arm into the rectums of fifty cows, one after another, to feel their uteruses for pregnancy—or to watch George rope, tie, and throw a bull to work on an infected foot. But surely the most breathtaking sight of all was watching George help deliver a calf. Over the months I have become a little casual about "preg checks" and George's roping skills, but the sight of a calf being born still lifts me right off the ground.

By the time I returned to the cabin about 6:30, both body and mind were completely exhausted. I sank into a chair and stared into the fire for what seemed like hours—until the sound of the telephone brought me back to conscious reality. It was George, calling from the hospital to say that there was an emergency accident case I might like to see. Something in the tone of his voice told me the day was far from over.

When I reached the hospital fifteen minutes later, George was in one of the examining rooms with a dog that had been hit by a car. Its jaw was completely broken and one eye was popping out of its socket. George needed an extra pair of hands, so there simply wasn't time for me to faint. A clot had formed behind the injured eye. I scrubbed my hands and held the animal while George took a syringe to see if he could draw off the clot. I managed somehow, more by concentrating on what needed to be done than by thinking about it. George then cleansed the eye, lubricated it, replaced it in the socket, and stitched the eyelids closed to hold it in place. Then he worked for more than half an hour to drill a hole through the jawbone so that it could be pinned and wired in place.

Driving back to the cabin I was beyond exhaustion. I also felt peaceful for the first time in many months. I knew that I was beginning to find some pieces of myself that had been lost. I had seen the power of a man who uses all his strength of body, which is considerable, and the sensitivity of his mind and heart to nurture and encourage growth and life.

14

I hope that the photographs that I have taken of my days with George will offer some insight into the dedicated life of a man I am honored to call my friend—and into the lives of many other large animal veterinarians like him. I have tried to create a typical day with George, but there really is no such thing. Few days are typical and none are routine.

At the end of the month of riding with George on his daily rounds, I returned to New York City with a new sense of personal strength and determination. It was time to get on with my own life, and I wanted to find a way of sharing my experiences. But whenever I feel down, whenever I feel blocked or trapped inside myself, no longer able to give in response to life, I head for Hillsdale, put on my coveralls and boots, and spend a few days working with George. Inevitably, while traveling the countryside, walking the fields, traipsing the barns and stables—"stomping out disease," as George laughingly puts it—the breathtaking wonder and challenge of life return.

Copake Veterinary Hospital   The Copake
Veterinary Hospital is located in Copake Falls, New York, about
fifty miles south of Albany. It is right on Route 22 and is surrounded
by mountains and farmland, fields and valleys of remarkable beauty
no matter the season. It is the place where George's day begins and
often ends.

Morning

George's day begins early. By 8:00 A.M. the three doctors—Layer, Jenkins, and Beneke—have gathered at the hospital in Copake to take morning calls.

Whoever has been on night duty was probably up at 4:00 A.M., the time when most farmers begin milking, taking an emergency call or two. There is no "night call" charge after 4:00 A.M. The vet's working day begins with the farmer's.

George doesn't seem to mind getting up early. It gives him a chance to see the sun rise. To George, that's something to see. There is a peacefulness about the early morning hours that makes it seem as if time were free.

At the hospital the three doctors divide up the calls and plan their morning rounds in the field. And they stop for a few moments, between answering the phones and loading up the three mobiles with fresh supplies, to consult on a troublesome case or share a new procedure.

Breakfast is often only a second or third cup of coffee.

Cows

Copake Falls, New York, is dairy country. George was born in nearby Millerton, on a dairy farm. His father, mother, and brother are dairy farmers. George is too—when he has the time. So it's no surprise that George really loves cows. When you ask him what it is that he likes most about cows, you can see a hundred different thoughts flashing through his head all at once—all of them important. But if you pin him down, he seems most impressed with their ability to take great pain and great stress and still survive and still produce. "You can cause them pain and five minutes later all is forgiven and they are back eating. They get on with it. That's how they survive—by getting on with it." George feels he's learned a lot from being around cows.

Interestingly, treating sick cows, and occasionally assisting in a difficult calving case, is not the most important service a veterinarian offers the dairy farmer. A cow doesn't just start producing milk automatically at two years of age. She has to be pregnant—and kept pregnant on a yearly cycle for maximum milk production. So one of George's major functions as veterinarian for dairy herds is helping the farmer determine precisely the right moment to breed the cow.

The best pregnancy cycle for a cow is a calf a year. And it is preferable, at least in the Northeast, for a cow to "freshen," or calve, in the fall of the year when milk prices are higher than they are in the spring, the more natural time for freshening. A cow's milk production reaches its peak about thirty to forty days after freshening and it remains high for the next six to eight months. If the cow has been rebred and is again pregnant, then about ten months after her first calf her milk supply "dries off" for two months, giving her a chance to store up energy and calcium for the new cycle. Since a cow's

21

gestation period is 305 days, ideally the cow is rebred 60 days after she freshens. That keeps her milk production at a yearly maximum without hurting the cow. A good milk-producing cow will give an astonishing 20,000 to 30,000 pounds of milk a year, even allowing for the two "dry" months.

Rectal examinations of the cow ("rectals," as George calls them) help George and the farmer determine precisely the right moment to breed the cow. In later rectals, by feeling the placenta and size of the uterus, George can verify that the cow is pregnant and, with considerable accuracy, tell the age and condition of the pregnancy. In a late rectal, he can sometimes actually feel the calf suck on his finger, a good sign. Fifty to a hundred rectals takes a strong arm.

Cows have four stomachs. The first stomach, the rumen, is a large fermentation vat of approximately sixty to seventy gallons of fluids and solid matter. The rumen is in almost constant motion and contains acids, bacteria, and yeast ("a beermaker's dream," according to George) which break down and modify the food the cow has foraged. The rumen is also, in a sense, part of the cow's natural defense mechanism. In the wild a cow is too heavy and too slow for protection against faster predators. She is in the open and vulnerable while grazing. Therefore, there is no time for chewing or breaking down food. Using her tongue as a big shovel, she grabs everything she can and then seeks a protected and safe spot for the long slow process of digestion to begin—in the rumen. The larger fibers are regurgitated, rechewed, and swallowed again until they are sufficiently broken down to pass through the rumen. Seeing a cow lying down in a field or barn chewing her cud is natural evidence of her serenity and good health.

You don't have to be around cows very long to fall in love with their beautiful faces and gentle eyes. George said to me one day, "Did you ever stop to think about eyes? Predators have eyes in the front of their heads. They only need to see their prey in front of them as they close in. But nonpredators have eyes in the sides of their heads; they need a wide circle of view to see what may be approaching from the side or behind. Man has eyes in front of his head. Think about that."

26

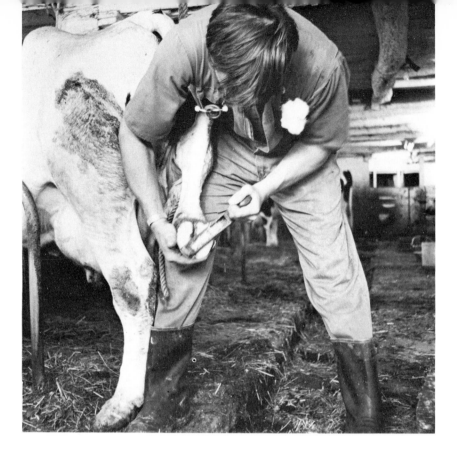

A cow's feet are trimmed and cared for whenever needed, but most often in the spring after long exposure to soft, muddy, and wet conditions.

The horns of a mature cow can be very dangerous both to people and to other cows in the herd. Most cows, especially in large herds, are routinely dehorned. Dehorning is best and most humanely done when the calf is one to three months old and the horns are not much larger than buttons. If the horns are allowed to develop, the nerve and blood supplies in the horns increase. The larger the horns are allowed to develop before dehorning, the greater the stress of the dehorning on the animal—and on the veterinarian.

Freestall barn

Stanchion barn

Milking parlor

Stress

As a veterinarian, George is constantly dealing with problems of stress as it affects animal health. To put it quite simply, stress is pressure—whether it is the physical pressure of an infected hoof or the emotional pressure of a strained environment. Stresses such as sore feet or sudden severe changes in temperature or feed are not necessarily harmful to the animal if treated promptly and effectively, but can be costly and seriously affect the milk production of a herd. And, like people, animals under stress are more susceptible to bacterial infection.

Emotional or environmental stress is often more subtle to detect and harder to treat. But it too can seriously affect the health and production of a herd. Interestingly enough, the basic design of the barn can often be the root cause of environmental stress. Whether a freestall barn or a stanchion barn (the two basic designs), the wrong farmer with the wrong barn can create a lot of stress on both his animals and himself.

In the freestall barn the cows are free to move about, eat when they choose, rest when they choose. At milking time they can be herded into the milking parlor, a dozen or more at a time. This is faster and more efficient than moving equipment from cow to cow, as is necessary in a stanchion barn where the cows are collared in place.

In stanchion barns, food is brought to each cow and her manure is carted away. It is much easier to spot a cow that is "off feed," one of the earliest symptoms of stress. It is also much easier to spot cows showing signs of heat, important in recognizing the right moment to breed them. In stanchion barns, greater attention can be given to individual animals, more likely to have names than numbers.

On the other hand, freestalls, if they are well designed, offer the animal a freer and more natural environment. That potentially means a lower level of stress—if the farmer is a good manager and a constant and sensitive observer of his animals.

Ideally, the design of the barn should match the temperament and management ability of the farmer. When it doesn't, there is very little that George can do about the stresses that arise except to treat symptoms. It's tough on the animals, tough on the farmer, and tough on the veterinarian.

Calving

"Storm comin' up. There'll be some calving cases tonight for sure." And for sure there were. There often seems to be a run of calving cases during storms and low pressure systems—not unlike the increase in the number of human births during the full moon. No one really knows why.

Most cows calve easily and naturally. But there are the hard cases—the breach births (hind feet first instead of head first), the oversized or deformed calves, or just plain difficult and long periods of labor. That's when the vet is called. In such cases, George usually goes into the birth canal to try to reposition the calf. Next he secures a chain around the calf's legs and then literally, with all his strength and the strength of two or three others, pulls the calf from its mother. Sometimes a special winch must be used. It may look cruel and harsh, especially on the calf, but calves are strong and fully formed at birth. They are commonly on their feet and walking within an hour.

Calves that must be pulled from the mother are often fine in spite of the ordeal, as in the case of the newborn twins on page 34. Other times, not even the shock of being thrown over a fence so that fluids suffocating the calf can drain from the lungs and trachea can revive a calf overstressed at birth. No veterinarian wins them all no matter how hard he tries. Losing a calf is a sad moment but you learn to live with it. You have to.

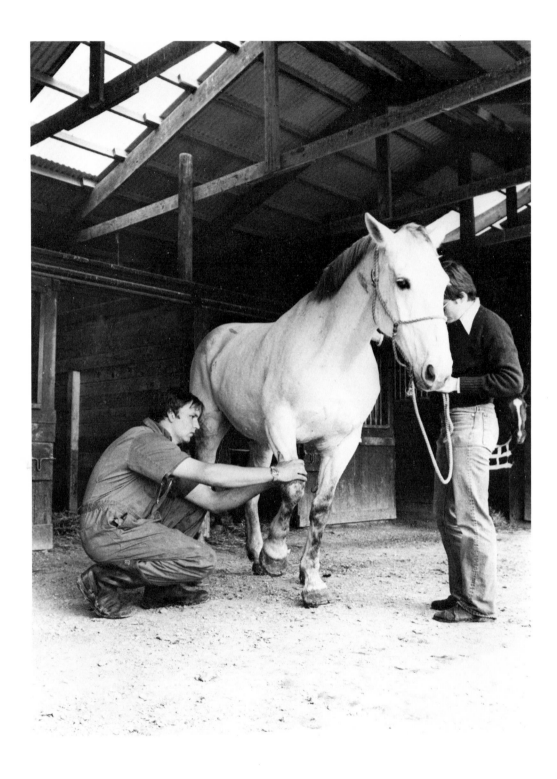

Pain

Animals can't tell you where it hurts, at least not directly. That means that George has to be acutely observant, has to find out for himself where and how much it hurts by actually trying to accentuate the pain in the suspected area. He prods, probes, presses—and carefully watches the animal's response. The response to pain is an especially important diagnostic technique when you can't talk to your patient.

A reverse technique, called "blocking," is often used on a horse that shows signs of being lame. After carefully examining the entire leg first, George can try to pinpoint the painful area by blocking—using a local anesthetic to deaden the feeling in one area. He begins the blocking at the hoof. If the stress is in the hoof, the local anesthetic will deaden the pain and when walked, the horse will no longer act lame. But if the horse still limps, then the pain is obviously higher in the leg and George blocks the next section, the fetlock, and continues blocking until the precise area of pain is located. X-rays may then be taken.

The ability to withstand pain, or pain tolerance, varies widely among animals and animal species. From his observations, George thinks that, in general, the more intelligent the species of animal, the less tolerant it is to pain. For example, you can see a cow dragging herself along on feet you know have got to be killing her. She may move slowly but she doesn't complain. Cows seem to have a high degree of pain tolerance. Horses, on the other hand, far more intelligent than cows, will often get "all bent out of shape," as George puts it, at just the sight of a vet with a needle.

Horse Clinic

In the springtime George sets up horse clinics for young horse owners at several central locations. George checks over the horse after a winter in the barn, files teeth, offers nutritional advice, gives the horse its tetanus and encephalitis shot, and takes a blood sample for the Coggins test. (The law requires that every horse be tested yearly for equine infectious anemia, a highly contagious disease.) Giving shots or taking a blood sample from a horse can be difficult. They are quick to sense what is coming and act up easily. The trick is in talking soothingly to the horse and not letting him catch sight of the needle before it comes. These horse clinics save George a lot of time and they save a young horse owner the cost of an individual call. As any horse owner will tell you, they are expensive pets. The clinics ease the burden on young owners and give George a chance to offer encouragement and help.

38

Inoculations

For about an hour after it is born a foal —or any baby for that matter—has the ability to absorb protective antibodies from its mother's milk, making it immune to all the things in the environment to which the mother has already developed an immunity, a natural immunity. Although the milk doesn't change for two or three days, the foal's ability to absorb antibodies lessens dramatically within an hour after birth. But for added protection, most foals are inoculated against tetanus and bacterial infection soon after birth.

Horse Castration

A horse is castrated to prevent him from becoming too excitable around the barn and to prevent him from possibly hurting himself by trying to break down a fence or stall to get to a mare in heat. Because of a horse's great susceptibility to tetanus, thorough sterile precautions are taken throughout the procedure.

Filing Teeth

In spring, the outer edges of the upper teeth and the inner edges of the lower teeth are often sharp. They are filed to prevent cheek and mouth sores from developing. It always looked a lot like brushing to me.

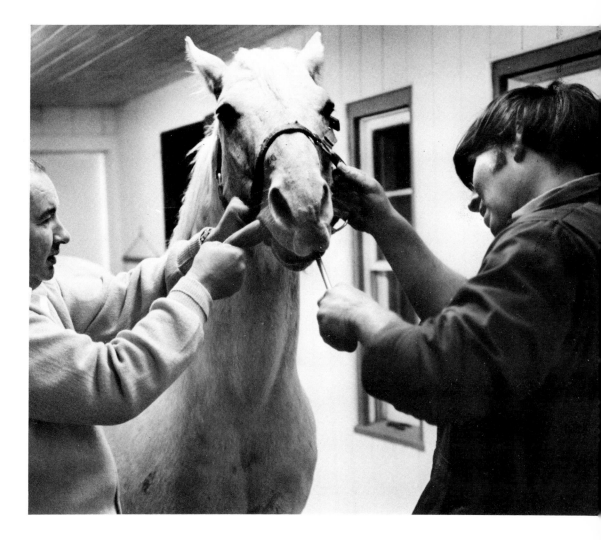

D.A. Field Operation

George wishes we had more field surgery pictures for the book—big time stuff. But the truth is that this simple D.A. (displaced abomasum) operation is not only fairly common, but one of the most strenuous in spite of its simplicity.

In a D.A., the cow's fourth stomach, the abomasum located near the midline of the lower abdominal cavity, floats out of place and up to one side. Years ago, the D.A. operation was more complicated because the abdominal cavity had to be opened up surgically. The cow was tied, thrown on her back, and further tied, much as the one in these pictures. The abomasum then floated back into place by the natural force of gravity. The abdominal cavity was then opened, and the abomasum was sewn securely into place. Then the abdominal cavity was sewn back up. This all had to be done quickly, in less than

42

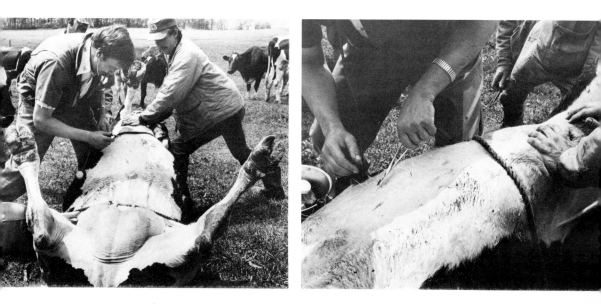

an hour, or the cow would suffocate from being kept on her back too long.

Today, George—and now many other vets—are using a much simpler procedure. And in fact, George was one of the first veterinarians to develop and encourage the technique. Instead of opening the abdominal cavity after the abomasum floats back into place, George uses a long, curved needle that penetrates both the cavity and the abomasum and sews them together. The simplicity of it still confounds a lot of farmers—and some veterinarians—used to the old procedure. And like any procedure, it is not always successful. But percentagewise, it is just as successful as the old way and it is less stressful on the cow. It is faster, and the cow is less likely to be in danger from suffocation. And there is no large incision. It also costs a lot less, which is helping to make it popular.

Piglet Castration

Male pigs are castrated at the age of three or four weeks . . . to make them more like females. Male meat, when developed, is tougher and has an odor; it doesn't taste as good. More fat is marbled into the meat of a castrated male; it is sweeter, more tender. It is part of the business.

A gaggle of geese!

Milk Plant

One morning we actually had time to stop for a coffee break. George pulled the mobile clinic up beside the old Millerton Milk Plant where the milk train used to stop . . . back in the old days. Every morning the farmers brought their milk in ten-gallon cans down to the milk plant, where it was weighed and put on the train for the city. While his milk cans were being steam washed, the farmer had time to stand around and jaw a bit with his neighbors, especially in the winter when there was less work to do around the farm and a hot cup of coffee was always welcome.

As George told me about the old days (he remembers going to the Millerton Milk Plant with his father as a kid back in the early 1950s—so the "old days" weren't so very long ago), it all sounded kind of nice to me. For sure, handling ten-gallon milk cans, maybe a hundred pounds each, was hard work. It amazes George that every farmer didn't have a hernia from lifting and carrying milk cans. Modern milking parlors and portable milking machinery, pipelines direct from the machinery to large cooling and storage tanks where the milk is picked up by large trucks—that's all a lot more efficient and a lot easier on the back.

We finished our coffee and drove away from the abandoned milk plant. We didn't say much. In our minds we were back in the old days . . . and a little reluctant to leave them behind.

Nursery School

George encourages everyone to respect and love animals, to learn about them, and to care for them properly. He's especially big on kids and one day he invited his son Chris's nursery school class down to the hospital to see what being a veterinarian is all about. The kids looked at fecal samples through the microscope and saw little wiggly things. They watched George perform a mock operation on a block of wood. They looked at an X-ray of a horse's leg. George showed them some of the tools he carries in the mobile and he opened his medical case. He showed them how he uses the mobile in the field and how he uses the two-way radio to talk to the hospital from the field or on the road. For the kids in Chris's class it was "Emergency" come to life, pretty high praise from four and five year olds. For George, it was the future learning about the present. It was also a lot of fun.

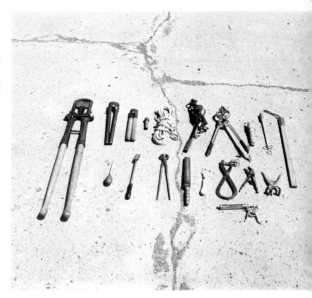

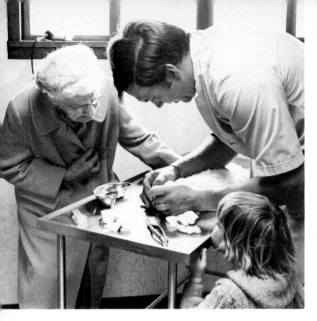

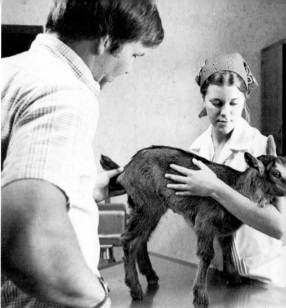

Examining a goat

Small Animal Office Hours George's young
daughter, Amy, stayed behind after the rest of the class to watch her
daddy remove some sore teeth from a cat.

Docking puppy dogs' tails

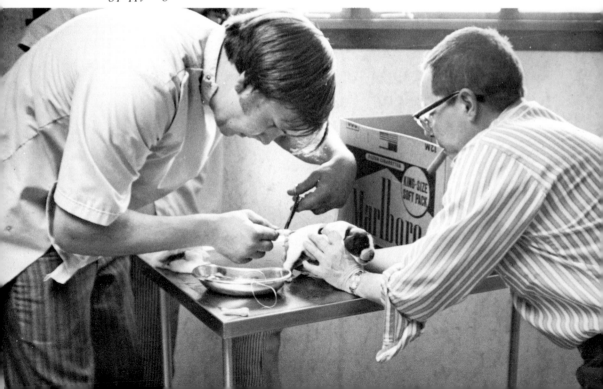

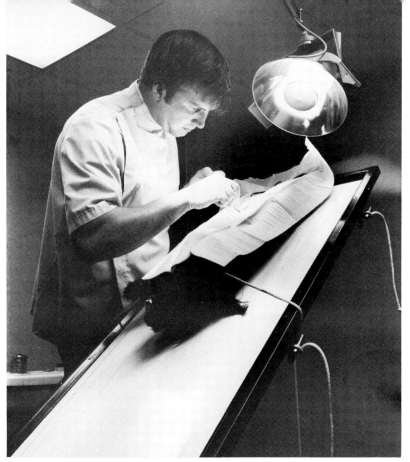

Surgery

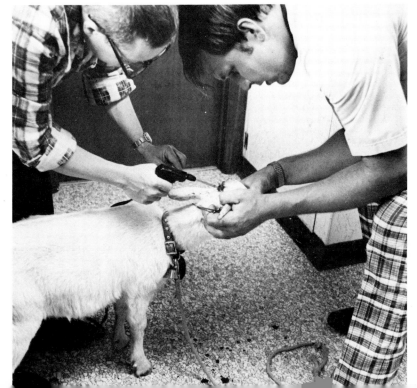

*Electrocauterizing
a wound*

Willow Brook

Willow Brook is the Beneke family dairy farm. George was born there in 1945 and, although he has a home and family of his own now, his roots are there. He stops by often—not just to visit family or treat the herd, but also to lend a hand or a back once in a while. George is a farmer at heart; he likes the idea that he can still go down and work the farm when he has time. It keeps him close to the land and the animals and it keeps him close to the daily problems of the other farmers he serves as a veterinarian. For George Beneke, at least, being a large animal veterinarian is being a farmer with a specialty in the care and treatment of animals.

54

Joe Beneke

George is very proud of his father, Joe Beneke, and they are very much alike—independent, hardworking, and practical. Joe Beneke came to the United States on his own as a boy of fourteen. He worked hard, determined to make his way. Eventually he saved enough to marry and buy a delicatessen in Brooklyn. More hard work. By 1944 he was able to sell the deli and buy Willow Brook, a proud moment. He was a farmer again, as his father and his grandfather had been in Germany. And he's been a farmer every day since, for nearly thirty-five years. Even though George's older brother, Henry, has now taken on many of the responsibilities for running Willow Brook, Joe Beneke still goes to work every day. His purpose and his pleasure are in his work. He can tell you from memory the sire, dam, and personal history of every cow in his 275-cow herd. And he's famous for the calves he raises. You can't tell Joe Beneke to stop working and take a rest any more than you can George.

Afternoon in the Field

It is not necessary to castrate a bull surgically, as it is a horse. A bull can be "clamped" with a pair of large pincers. Every man who watches a "clamping" feels it very personally.

John is one of George's favorite herdsmen. His presence in any barn would do a lot of good.

Passing a tube through the nose of a badly dehydrated horse on into the stomach is a way of giving fluids in large volumes. It is also a way of making sure the stomach isn't twisted. And it is one way of worming.

A cat gets its temperature taken on an informal examining table.

"Ringing" a bull—putting the bull ring through the bull's nostrils—can be very touch and go. One wrong touch and you go.

Mastitis and milk fever are two problems that account for many of George's cow calls. Milk fever occurs when a cow loses too much calcium during and immediately after calving. She puts all the calcium she can into the calf and into her milk, exhausting her own supply. She goes down under extreme stress. She is given a calcium and dextrose pickup intravenously.

Mastitis is an inflammation of the udder caused by a bacterial infection in the milk gland. If not treated in time, the infection can become systemic, spilling into the cow's whole system. It can dry up one or more of the udder's four quarters, cutting off milk production. Mastitis is difficult to control, and few farms have no mastitis cases. Milk fever and mastitis often occur together, the mastitis bacteria (almost always present at some level) attacking and taking hold when the cow is already weakened with milk fever.

A Detective Story

This cow was in really bad shape when we arrived—dehydrated, diarrhea all over the place, heaving, she couldn't get up; she was obviously in great pain. After quickly getting her started on fluids and antibodies, (essential no matter what the problem), George began to look around. The cow was having a violent reaction to something. But what? Instinctively, he began to wonder if she could have gotten into some kind of poison. Her symptoms would fit. He checked the trash around the barn for car batteries, paint cans, insecticides, solvents, gasoline, fertilizer ... carelessly left where an animal could get into them. Cows especially are indiscriminate eaters. George didn't find anything obvious around the barn.

There was another puzzle. If it was some kind of poison, why weren't at least a couple other cows affected? She was the only one down. George started to walk out into the pasture where the cows had been grazing. It was spring. Some plants are very toxic in the

spring. But if there were toxic or poisonous plants in the pasture, there should have been more than one cow down. Could she have wandered off by herself, developed a taste for a plant the rest ignored? We walked a ways farther and then George bent over and pulled a weed. We looked around and some of the nearby weeds were chomped off as if they had been eaten. George looked at the weed in his hand carefully. "That's veratrum. I think that's what's troubling her." After two days of fluids and antibodies, the cow just barely made it.

Poisoning cases are not nearly as common in the Northeast as they are in the Southwest, but occasionally a cow will get into veratrum or one of the many other poisonous plants. Some just develop a liking. George urges his farmers to be especially careful about keeping the late summer pastures mowed, to keep the weeds down. In August and September the fields start to dry down and animals start to run out of things to eat. You don't want them eating just any old weed.

Horse Down

This is one of the most difficult pictures I've ever taken. I'm not sure I even wanted to take it at the time. It is an invasion and intrusion on a deep and private pain.

E.I.A.—equine infectious anemia—or just plain "swamp fever," as it is commonly known, is one of the most dreaded of all horse diseases because there are no known protective immunities against it and it is usually fatal. It is spread by flies and mosquitoes and so it spreads easily. Once it gets started, it can quickly turn into an epidemic. Since a horse can be what is known as a "carrier" and harbor and spread the disease without showing any symptoms itself, the law requires that owners have their horses blood-tested yearly. If a horse tests positive—shows it has the disease—it must either be totally and permanently isolated, screened away at all times, which is impossible when you start to think about it . . . or put down.

Tests on two horses taken a few days earlier at the horse clinic came back positive. George was called to put them down. It was late afternoon, the last call of the day, barring emergencies. That kind of a call is never easy, and it seems particularly hard at the end of the day. But it had to be done. As if preparing himself for the difficult moments ahead, George told me about a case of swamp fever that turned into an unusually sad story.

A horse had tested positive, showing that it was a carrier. It belonged to a young girl who had grown up on it, raising and caring for it. The girl's parents didn't want her told and wouldn't allow the horse to be put down; they were trying to protect her from a harsh reality. Six months later another horse farther down the road caught the disease and died. Then the girl had to be told and her horse put down. She had to face not only the loss of her own horse, but the probability that her horse had passed the disease on to a neighbor's horse.

Everything I knew in my head about the rightness and humaneness of what I was about to see didn't make it any easier. A deep hole had been prepared in the field by a bulldozer. It kept filling up with mud and water, trying to level itself . . . almost as if in protest. Each horse, each beautiful, spirited horse would be led to the edge of the ditch; George would quickly inject 30 ccs. of euthanasia solution into the neck. Within seconds it would stagger and collapse dead, shoved into the ditch as it fell.

It was an incredible, private agony for everyone there, but most especially for the two young women who had loved those horses a lot of years. It must have been unbearable for them to lead their horses to that ditch. I saw a lot of agony . . . and a lot of courage.

We rode back to the hospital in silence.

EFFECT ON ANIMAL:

LOWERED RESISTANCE ⟶ PREY TO OTHER

LESS APPETITE ⟶ LESS WEIGHT GA

BODY FUNCTIONS
LESS EFFICIENT ⟶ POOR CONVERSION
INTO NEW TISSUE

EMIA ⟶ WEAKNESS, EMAC

Teaching

To George, being a country vet is a bigger responsibility than simply the treatment of sick animals. He feels that he must also be a teacher, that he must help every owner understand his or her animal's sickness and exactly how to care for it properly. The health of the animal depends as much on the owner as it does on him.

One night a week for a series of weeks, he teaches a veterinary science class at the high school. The class is for high school students, but many of their parents attend with them. After class George stays around until every question is asked—and answered to the best of his ability.

George is also a leader in the 4-H Club program. At the annual 4-H Club Round-Up, youngsters are eased into the art of grooming and showing the calves they have raised and cared for themselves. I asked George once why he gave so much of his time to teaching. His answer was simple: "In veterinary medicine you share with everyone."

Fairs Traditionally, fairs are times when farm families get together and compete just for the fun of a good time—and let loose a little after the hay crop is in. It's also a good chance to see how the other guy is doing, challenging you to go back and improve your herd.

66

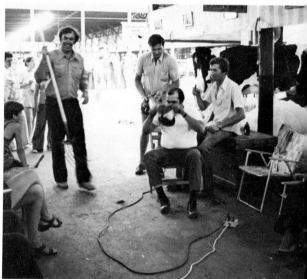

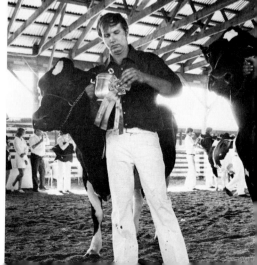

Garden

For a large animal vet, there's very little spare time. But in spring and summer, George looks forward to spending what little there is in his garden—a family project with his wife, Cathy, and children, Chris and Amy. George is proud of his well-composted, highly organic soil. Enriching the soil gives him more pleasure than counting the number of tomatoes he can produce. He sums it up this way: "The way you go about gardening, the way you go about farming, the way you go about anything is a lot more important than what you produce, or how many pounds of gain to pounds of feed you produce, or how many calls you knock off in one day."

To George, the whole of our environment is very much like the soil in his garden. You enrich it, it enriches you. You contribute to it whatever you can. You keep it healthy and productive, and it will support and sustain life for all creatures in abundance.

68

How Louis Got His Name

This book wouldn't be complete without a picture of Louis (pronounced Louie). And in fact, I took quite a few pictures of Louis, at least I thought they were of Louis—only to learn that black labs are pretty common in the country. Actually, I had gotten good pictures of Sam next door and even better ones of Ben down the road. But none of Louis, until we took this one.

George explained to me once how Louis got his name. When George was in vet school at Cornell, vet students made the decision as to which dogs would be used in pharmacology experiments. The dogs were acquired from the pound. The year before, the class ahead of George had "pulled the plug" on a black lab named Louis two or three times; they saved him from more than one fatal experiment. "Everybody knew Louis. Everyone knew to leave him alone. He'd even go into the classrooms whenever he wanted. He was Mr. Cool. I really loved him."

The first September after George graduated and began practicing, he saved a four-month-old black lab from a trip to the pound and brought him home. That's how this Louis got his name—and how the Benekes got a best friend.

A Cow Lick
I call this picture of George's daughter *A Cow Lick for Amy*. It reminds George of his own childhood. "I guess I was about six or seven when I first knew that I wanted to be a vet. I remember standing in a box stall with a cow down with milk fever, waiting for the vet to come. I kept thinking, 'I ought to be able to treat her myself. That way I wouldn't have such a helpless feeling.' " It took years of hard work and long years of schooling to reach that goal. Was it worth it I asked him one day? His answer: "I have never gotten over the thrill of being a veterinarian."

71

To be a veterinarian requires:

2 years, minimum, of a college preveterinary program

4 years of veterinary medical school, the fourth year being
basically an intern program

Licensing by the state (or states) in which you practice

The preparation is long and difficult. Just wanting to be a veterinarian is not enough. The competition to get into one of the
twenty-one veterinary medical schools in the United States is stag-
gering. According to the latest figures of the American Veterinary
Medical Association, in 1976 the combined freshman classes totalled
only 1,856 students, 15 percent of the number of qualified applicants.
It is a high honor just to be accepted. In recent years there has been a
steady increase in the number of women entering the profession; 28
percent of the 1976 freshman classes were women.

Seventy-six percent of veterinary medical school graduates go into
private practice. Others go into research, teaching, government
service, public health, and the military. Of the 76 percent that do go
into private practice, 46 percent go into exclusively small animal
practices, 9 percent go into exclusively large animal practices, and 46
percent go into combined large and small animal practices such as
George Beneke's.

For further information write:

American Veterinary Medical Association
930 North Meacham Road
Schaumburg, Illinois 60196

Ask for a free copy of the pamphlet, *Today's Veterinarian.* Enclose a
stamped, self-addressed envelope.

The Veterinarian's Oath

Being admitted to the profession of veterinary medicine, I solemnly dedicate myself and the knowledge I possess to the benefit of society, to the conservation of our livestock resources and to the relief of suffering animals. I will practice my profession conscientiously with dignity. The health of my patients, the best interests of their owners, and the welfare of my fellow man, will be my primary considerations. I will, at all times, be humane and temper pain with anesthesia where indicated. I will not use my knowledge contrary to the laws of humanity, nor in contravention to the ethical code of my profession. I will uphold and strive to advance the honor and the noble traditions of the veterinary profession. These pledges I make freely in the eyes of God and upon my honor.

Richard B. McPhee, a free-lance photographer and writer, shares his New York City apartment with a Great Dane and two cats. But their hearts are in the country and they never miss an opportunity to head for the farm.

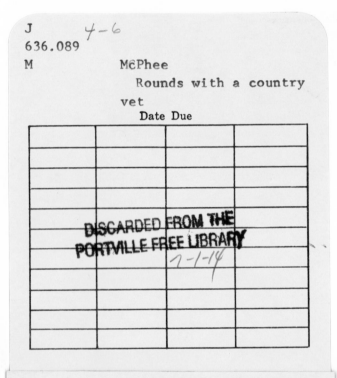